Gary:

Good luck &
Good Head!

OFF-THE-WALL

May all your *Bozos*
be Wall-Huggin'!

[signature]

OFF-THE-WALL
A GRADUATE COURSE IN DEER HUNTING

JACK VAN RIPER

CHIPPEWA ADVENTURES
DURAND, MICHIGAN

Additional copies of this book may be ordered
through bookstores or by sending $12.95 plus $3.50
for postage and handling to:

Publishers Distribution Service
6893 Sullivan Road
Grawn, MI 49637
(800) 507-2665

Publisher's Cataloging-in-Publishing Data

Van Riper, Jack, 1935-
    Off the wall: a graduate course in deer hunting/
by Jack Van Riper.–
Chippewa Adventures, Durand, Michigan
        p.   ill.   cm.
Includes index.
        ISBN: 0-9643001-0-9
        1. White-tailed deer hunting - Michigan. 2. Deer hunting -
        Michigan.
I. Title.
SK301.V36   1994
799-27'7357–dc20   94-72441

Manufactured in the United States of America

10 9 8 7 6 5 4 3 2 1

Book Design by Debra Anton / PDS.

This book is dedicated to my Lord and
Savior, JESUS CHRIST. He gave
me one more chance!

≥ Contents ≥

➵ INTRODUCTION ➵

There is so much about the pursuit of the white tailed buck, that does not fall within the bounds of normalcy, I thought a book of the odd-ball things these critters do to evade you and me, might just help increase our success.

I have included many of the strange places these wearers of antlers may hang out and some of the more novel ways in which your brothers of the brush have employed to put their heads on the wall.

I sincerely hope that the reading of this book will help you as much as the writing has helped me. Several of the ideas set forth herein have been responsible for my taking bragging size bucks, and nearly every idea has resulted in some hunter bagging a buck for the book or a horn for a hat rack.

Whether it be venison for the table or antlers for the wall, this collection of ideas is put forth to make you think and to make you a better hunter. Dive in and let your imagination run rampant; you never know, the idea you get could just put the biggest buck you have ever seen right square in your sights the next time out.

Join us in hunting big bucks, OFF-THE-WALL!

A Super Off-The-Wall Buck
The present State Record 6-point

DISCLAIMER

Nothing that you are about to read in this book, is intended by the author to be a suggestion, that you the reader, should violate or break any Local, State or Federal Laws.

Neither is it suggested, that you do anything illegal, immoral or fattening in your pursuit of the elusive "superbuck".

However, you will note in your reading, that the OFF-THE-WALL bucks we talk about, operate without any such constraints. The whitetailed deer is no respecter of man's trespass laws, or of the government's many rules and regulations.

While we must learn to work within and around these legal and moral constraints, our adversary will be using them to keep his antlers off our walls. The author recognizes these problems and hopes, with your recognition will come solutions and that these help you gain an advantage in the game of trophy hunting!

OFF-THE-WALL

The Land

E veryone has to be somewhere and all the "super bucks" I know of live on the land. The land may differ from swamp to semi-desert, or from flat farm land to hilly mountains, but everywhere there is land there is a whitetailed buck, just waiting to pull some off-the-wall maneuver, to keep his antlers off your wall.

A whitetail buck lives on the land 24 hours of the day and because of this he knows it better than you do; that is a given. However, as well as he knows his land, you have one distinct advantage, you are smarter! At times you will doubt your mental brilliance, but if you will just stretch your brain cells on a regular basis, you will begin to out think and out maneuver even the shiftiest hat rack! That is the reason I have written OFF-THE-WALL, to help you stretch those mental muscles. Learn to think weird, wacky and whitetail, learn to think, OFF-THE-WALL!

When we go looking for "super bucks" we seldom take a stand in the middle of a bare field or any other piece of land without natural cover, but we are wrong. Big bucks get to be big bucks because they live longer and they live longer because they travel routes that provide little space for ambush.

They know that they are safe, when they are out in the middle of a 40 acre hay field and they know it is safe to cross that bean field, smack dab in the middle. They've been doing so for years and they know it's safe. That's the secret, they have been doing it for years and no one has bothered them—habit, safe habit.

Look for tracks, big tracks. Look for tracks in the mud, in the sand, in the snow in the morning & in the evening. The big guy, as well as the little guy, can not go anywhere without leaving a track. Somewhere he has a favorite way to cross the land, find it and you are on your way to putting him on your wall. You'll read this again and again. **Keep a book on each buck**, soon you will see a pattern.

I know one successful southern Michigan hunter who has taken three record book bucks from in back of his father-in-law's barn, right smack in the middle of his cow pasture. All three bucks were dropped within 40 yards of each other. Here there is no more cover than 3 inches of grass and a scattered bull thistle or three. He sits in a little depression he has hollowed out of the ground and drops these biggies as they move from one cornfield to another. They are moving along a little sag in the ground.

For those of you that don't know, a sag is a natural depression in an otherwise flat piece of ground. Sometimes this sag is so inconspicuous that you can be right in the middle of it and not know it. The deer know where the sags are, it is where they can cross without being seen or without seeing danger.

My friend made this observation by reading tracks in the snow one winter and then confirming it the following summer, when he was setting in a far away tree and watching his first "super buck" follow that sag. A little spade work and he was in place when opening day came.

Similar to a sag, is a bowl or depression. While these are seldom used as travel routes, they are used as resting places. These spots can, at times, hold the biggest bucks around. Especially when does are in estrus.

There is one such depression, not far from my home in

Mid-Michigan. It is located right in the middle of a
section, at it's highest point and can't be seen from any
road. I only know it is there, because the landowner told
me that every time he goes to that field, he finds deer
bedded down in the middle of it. We've had no hits, but
several runs and numerous errors trying to get at these
critters. One of these days we are going to get a
combination of crops in this section that will allow us to
approach this spot. Why the special interest? Because
there is a 160 plus "wall hanger" that sometimes visits
there and you never know when he'll make a mistake.

I know one outstanding hunter, with multiple record
book trophies to his credit, that has for years been
working on a buck so big, that he uses 12 inch and better
trees for his rubbing posts. This buck uses as his
stomping ground, a pothole in the middle of a 400 acre
cornfield.

Our hunter stumbled on this spot one winter after the
corn was picked. He hunted it many times, but was never
able to catch the buck with his guard down. Apparently
the buck only visited this spot after dark and then circled
the pothole to check the wind before considering that
place safe. By the size of the tracks and the size of the
rubs, my friend thinks this "wall hanger" could be a new
state record.

Potholes have long been known as good places to jump
big bucks, but all to often this jumping results in nothing
more than a glimpse of a fast disappearing white tail and
any shot taken is chancy at best. Potholes come in many

descriptions, large and small, wet or dry. They can be right out in the open or buried in the center of a big grain field. To hunt these features of the land successfully, generally requires more than one hunter and some preparation is usually necessary. Try to always remember this saying when going after one of these "wall hangers". "Prior Planning Prevents Piss-Poor Performance".

You may stumble on the location of a trophy buck, but you will seldom stumble on him twice in the same place. Big bucks hide out in places where they are not bothered, like potholes. However, when they are once run out of one of their lay-ups, it will generally be a week or more before they return to that spot to hide once again.

When he no longer feels secure he'll move on to another of his hideouts and believe me, he has more than one. I suspect that some big bucks never return to a spot they have been jumped from, at least not during the same season. As I have said before: **Keep a book on where he travels and where you jump him**. You may not see him in the same pothole again this year, but next year, with a little prior planning, you may be standing right where he exits that hay field, after your partner kicks him out of his pothole bed. Don't forget the six "P's".

The opposite of sags, and bowls and depressions are hills and knobs and ridges. Mountains can be and are another whole system of their own and we won't cover them here. I only have experience with them in New England and in Michigan's U.P. and know of no off-the-wall system for hunting them that probably isn't already familiar to you.

When the going gets tough, the bucks get going,
to the top of this hill in northern Michigan.

Hills in the Midwest can be as small as a 10 foot up-thrusting in the middle of an otherwise flat field, or a 200 to 300 foot swelling that covers 4 or 5 square miles. Wherever that hill may be, it is sure to see it's share of whitetailed visitors.

Knobs are peculiar to a special place in the Midwest, mainly Wisconsin and Kentucky. Generally speaking knobs are one to two hundred foot, steep sided protuberances from 100 to 300 feet across at the top. The top can be either flat or rounded and the sides gullied or brush covered. Knobs can be hunted the same as any large hill and the same precautions should be taken. However, if the knob is smallish, great care must be taken with regards to noise. A broken stick on one side of a small knob might be easily heard on the other side.

I know you are familiar with hills and have probably

hunted in and around them all of your life, but there are some very special relationships that male whitetails have with hills. If I may remind you of some of these relationships it may make bagging one of these bucks much easier.

Where possible, bucks like to lay up just under the crest of a hill, with the wind at their back and a clear view of the landscape to their front. **Don't ever forget this, he won't.**

Where large trees are present, he will select his bed in the hollow at the base of one of these trees. Knowing this will allow you to plan your approach so as to come at him from the side or across wind. Sometimes it is possible, through the use of binoculars or a spotting scope, to set afar off and pin point his location. Once this is known, you can then plan your stalk, so as to take advantage of that location's weakness.

I'm not exactly sure that every location has a weakness. For years I worked on a Big Rapid's big buck, with a set up just like this and all I ever got to see of him was his tail, 3 times. He had chosen a very steep maple, beech and tag alder covered hill, skirted on the West by a two track and on the East by an elm swamp. Reasonable access could only be gained by coming up the Southwest end from the road or up the North end, through a tangle of "tags". The East side of the hill was nearly unclimbable, what with its steepness and slippery covering of leaves. About a third of the way from the Northern end, on the East side, a small spur tapered down and around, the end of the swamp.

The swamp was a prime hiding spot for hard pressed deer and contained several scrapes, along trails that criss-crossed it. One year it would be wet, the next dry. Nonetheless, deer used it all the time.

This buck always had a scrape and licking branch, under a lone tag alder, right on the very top of the hill. I always found his bed 20 yards down its East face, usually on the spur. With the prevailing wind normally from the west/southwest you could seldom approach him from any direction other than the North.

Two of the three times I saw parts of him, I was coming in from that direction and he bailed out into the swamp. Once on a still day I spent the better part of an hour climbing the southwest end and caught him tending a doe at the scrape. Before I could separate him from the doe, they both bolted down the north slope and I was left looking again.

One obvious ploy that I tried, that didn't work, was getting into position well before daylight. If it had worked I would have caught him returning from his nightly rounds. The three times I tried this, he never showed. Either he was somewhere else those times, or he was completely nocturnal as to his approach to this bedding area. He may have caught me coming in, after he was already there.

My point in all of this is, year in and year out, big bucks

pick spots like this for their lay-up's and if you will just recognize them in your hunting territory, you sometimes can outsmart and outthink them and put them on your wall. Then again, there are those bucks that are, forever lucky!

The last time I hunted that piece of Big Rapid's property was 1984 and in the meantime it has changed hands. You know what? Even though someone else owns it, I'd bet there is still a big buck using the same tactics on that same old hill. It's just the kind of place an off-the-wall buck likes!

Another slick use of the land by deer, is a hill just west of town. Here the farmer is able to farm the top and all of the slopes, except for a narrow strip of crest about 10 feet wide, just on the East side. This hill is about 100 feet high and over looks an old state highway, which sees a lot of traffic between two small towns. Time and time again I've looked up this hill as I've been passing by and there would be two or three deer laying down watching the road. One was usually a buck.

Once again the prevailing wind was at their back, the road was on the South and the farmers home and buildings were 300 yards across the flat part of the field to the North. An approach from the road would have been possible, except that it was all heavily posted and the posting was enforced.

These deer knew they were safe and they used this spot often. Because I've observed this spot being used over a period of several years, it is obvious that this information is being passed on from one generation to another of whitetails. And we thought we were the only species that had an information explosion.

As the last little tidbit in this chapter, I want you to remember that as a rule whitetail bucks like to lay up high. If there is a hill or ridge or high spot in their territory that is generally where they will choose for their daytime resting place. Even in a swamp they will usually pick the highest spot.

Veteran cedar swamp hunters know, that if they can find a ridge even two feet above the normal swamp bottom, they have found the bed and travel route of nearly every buck using that particular swamp. This also holds true for any other type of swamp or depression. It would seem that nearly everything likes to look down on danger. Even cattail bucks will seek out the highest spot in a cattail marsh.

SUMMARY

CHAPTER 1: The Land

A. All the "super bucks" live somewhere and that is on the land.

B. A buck may know the land better, but you are smarter.

C. Learn to think off-the-wall, learn to think whitetail.

D. Look for and find big tracks. He can not go anywhere without leaving tracks.

E. KEEP A BOOK ON EACH OF YOUR BUCKS. Soon you will see a pattern.

F. Big bucks tend to relate to land forms such as:
   1. sags
   2. bowls/depressions
   3. potholes
   4. hills/knobs/ridges
   5. swamps

G. Big bucks like to lay up high with the wind at their back.

H. Prior Planning Prevents Piss-Poor Performance
   Scout   Scout   Scout

Woods and Weather;
Fence Rows and Funnels

F or many years the pursuit of whitetailed bucks meant taking to the woods and woodlots, because that was where they lived. They still do live in the woods, but that is not an off-the-wall place to hunt them, it is instead the normal place. The one off-the-wall thing we must remember about wooded areas is, the bigger they are, the bigger are the deer that may come from them.

Big deer come from big woods, because they have a larger track of land to lose themselves in. Any time you have a piece of woodland unbroken by roads for 2 to 3 miles and a mile or more in thickness you have an ideal place for a super buck to grow big and develop some real off-the-wall habits.

The number one big buck tactic, as we have covered it in the first chapter, is laying up high or low with the wind at his back. If he can smell you coming from one way and see you coming from another you are going to have a tough time getting to him from the other directions, unless you know where he is in that woods or woodlot. In a wood or wood lot he can also be tipped-off to your presence by other animals in the woods, such as squirrels and birds.

Just to start your search for a truly off the wall buck get a good county map at your County Court House and look for double and triple sections without roads through them and then go for a drive. Look for those areas that have big woods, swamps or hills in those unbroken sections. When you have located an area where these conditions are present, you have found the home of a super buck or two. Remember, just because you have never seen this "rocking chair runner", it does not mean that he isn't there. I know of no location, that meets the above criteria that doesn't have at least one whitetail buck that will make the record books; most have two or three!

A county map, plat book and note book.
Necessary tools in any trophy hunters bag of tricks!

Once you have singled out one of these special areas, you should first of all secure permission from the land owner to hunt on his land. You can find out who to contact by purchasing a Plat Book from your County Co-op Extension Office. These books list all of the property owners on a township map and show their names and the amount of acreage they own. It will also show any State or Federal land.

It has been my experience, that once I have permission, I actually do a better job of scouting and hunting. For you young hunters and for you first time older hunters, I cannot stress enough the advisability of getting to know the farmers and landowners in your hunting area. Not only is having permission the law in my State of Michigan, but it is the very life blood of hunting throughout most of these United States. Without the cooperation of these fine men and women, who allow us the use of their land, we just wouldn't have much of a sport at all.

Once by accident and by being observant, I discovered how deer in general use a woods in inclement weather. In this case I was driving across the state on an October day, during a rotten piece of weather, and had the opportunity to check my theory on several dozen woodlots and woods. I could not verify this theory on every woodlot that I observed, but at nine (9) of them, I found deer laying on the side away from the wind and rain.

This knowledge that I stumbled on, along with some other that you may have picked up through the years, might just tip the scales in your favor some time.

When a storm is approaching from the West the deer in a medium or small woodlot will all move to the far East side of the wood and lay down facing the East. Once again this puts the wind at their back and open land to their front. It also puts the woods between them and the storm and makes life warmer, dryer, and safer. Also, less trees fall on the side away from the storm than fall on the side where natures full fury has a chance to work.

If you are in a woods when a storm hits be especially watchful, big bucks do not like to be caught out in a storm any more than you do. If they are away from their home base they will almost always try to get to one of their hiding spots before the full fury strikes. Once again, **keep a book on your bucks and your territory**, know your land as well as you can. Use your head, if the Weather Channel says there is a chance for a front to move through tomorrow plan to hunt in cover on the side away from the approaching storm. Your chances for a shot will double if you pick the right side.

Woodland hunting, before and during a big storm is best done near the heaviest cover in or near that woods. For instance a cedar swamp, heavy pine thicket or tag alder tangle. Deer seem to have a weather sense that tips them off when a storm is coming. First they will feed, then they will hit the bushes and lay up till it is past.

Just because there is a storm approaching or because it is raining is no reason to stay out of the woods.

Of course, you must be reasonable and not go into the tall timber during a lighting storm, but the deer are there all the time and my observation has been that as soon as the rain stops the big guys are out and about refreshing their scrapes. If you hope to ambush a biggie when his guard is down this is a prime time to do so.

I can remember sitting in a wet old ditch next to the road, waiting for my wife to pick me up one afternoon in late October, with a surprise thunder storm crackling lighting all around. I thought it was going to be my last hunt there was so much lighting. As luck would have it my wife was late and as the last boom of thunder rumbled off to the East here came the biggest buck I had seen that year, pussy footing down the edge of the woods checking and refreshing every scrape. Just as he reached the point where he was going to turn and present me with a shot opportunity, my wife pulled up and sounded the horn. I don't know if it was the horn or my cursing that scared that one into the next county, but he did teach me a lesson. The lesson, that has resulted in the taking of several of his kin is: Big bucks like bad weather; learn to use it to your advantage.

Weather has another effect on the big guys, it helps lay your scent. In other words it catches it on the rain drops or snow flakes and carries it to earth and out of the air currents. I know this is a fact because I have had many deer walk by me within 20 yards down wind during light rain and snow without so much as a sniff. This may not be conclusive to you, but it makes sense to me.

The old rule that scent will rise up a slope in the morning and sink down a slope in the evening, when there is no other appreciable air movement, is also true. Once again 45 years of deer hunting have proven this true, the hard way; missed deer because they smelled me before I could shoot.

Foggy weather is much the same as wet weather, it seems to lay the scent. It is interesting to note that a foggy day is an excellent day to hunt big bucks. Number one, they are unable to smell you, #2, because of the fog, they can't see you as well and #3, the fog also dampens the grass and leaves and makes hearing less acute. A foggy day is a good time to make an assault on the big guys secret hide out.

Remember, keep a book on your big bucks and the territory, so when a magic day appears, you will be ready.

It was a wet/windy day when this non-typical
fell to this lucky Southern Michigan hunter.

Windy weather is perhaps the worst time to hunt most deer, because when the wind is gusty the deer are very nervous. They have a reason to be nervous, they are unable to hear as well and scent is blown all over the place confusing their otherwise first line of defense. In this type of weather deer will often seek out open grassy fields and let their eyes do most of the work in protecting them. They also use corn and bean fields in this type of weather and in the big woods huckleberry bogs, and cedar swamps.

We'll talk about hunting corn fields in the chapter on crops, but a slow careful stalk on a windy day has put many a big buck off their range and on the wall, regardless of the place they have picked to hide.

FUNNELS

Fence rows and funnels have much in common, because many times fence rows act as a principle ingredient in whitetail funnels; first of all let's define a funnel. Yea, I know you know what a funnel is, but let us just redefine it so we are all on the same page to start with. Number one (1), I didn't find a good description of a funnel in the dictionary, at least not a good one for us to use, so I've made up my own.

A funnel is an instrument or contrivance, (1) made of paper, plastic, metal or wood used in the transferring of a pourable material or liquid from one container to another, (2) used to facilitate the moving of material or things from a larger container or area into another or smaller area or container. As in; the combination of the two fence rows and the drainage ditch, did much to funnel the local population of whitetails into a road crossing, right at the north edge of our property.

O.K., we now have a place to start. Funnels are either man-made or natural and serve to cause deer to act in a predictable fashion when they encounter them. This is where funnels help us put those off-the-wall bucks, on our walls.

Wildlife funnels can cause a constriction of deer travel routes from several, over many miles or acres, down into one or two in a very small area. By learning to identify the location of these constrictions or squeezes we can find the absolute best spot to place our stand or the best place to be waiting when a drive is being conducted.

Some truly outstanding whitetail trophy buck hunters, such as Owosso, Michigan's, Jack Eddy, with 11 super bucks in the Commemorative Bucks of Michigan, Inc, record book, have turned locating these funnels and using them into a science.

Jack Eddy of Owosso
and two of his recent
Michigan trophy bucks.

I'm not nearly as good as Jack Eddy, but here are some of the important points in using fence rows and funnels to harvest those big bruisers.

As we stated in the first chapter, get to know your land. **Keep a book on your big buck and your territory.** Spend time driving the roads in your hunting area and make a special note of where deer trails cross. Look for natural funnels such as narrow wood lines and brushy draws that provide cover almost to the road on either side. Deer will sometimes go a long way out of their way to use these natural features when the only alternative is crossing large tracts of open ground. When you find such a location in conjunction with a well used game trail you have found a funnel.

Other, not so apparent, funnels deal with terrain features such as ridges , water, valleys and crops.

Deer, and in particular bucks, love to follow ridge tops in their travels and will continue to follow these tops even when they funnel down and cross roads. Generally speaking when these ridges meet a road there will be a cut-bank on either side of the road. Look for the main crossing spot a little to either side of this steep place. My experience has been that the big bucks will cross 20 to 40 yards further down the slope or to the side of the main crossing.

There is a general rule for bucks; they seldom run the main trails, but take a route several yards to either side. If possible it will be on the downwind side. Locate the main trail or funnel route and then look for the big buck route off to one side or off-the-wall. Keep a book on your big buck and on your territory.

Some of you may be able to carry a complete picture in your mind of all the landscape in your hunting territory. Unfortunately, most of us are incapable of achieving this state of intelligence, we must rely on a county map or an aerial photo. The aerial photo is the best because you can actually see the funnels. Sometimes you're able to see obvious funnels that you have overlooked from your on ground observations.

Aerial photo of a funnel by Terry Kemp

Another of my record book friends from Owosso, Terry Kemp and a long time hunting buddy, will go so far as to charter a flight in a small plane and take his own pictures of an area containing a book buck. When he adds to this information, a county map with his personal notations, he has a valuable blue print for the harvesting of an off-the-wall buck. Aerial photos of a county may be seen at most County Zoning Offices or at the Cooperative Extension Office. Copies of these photos can sometimes be purchased from those organizations or a local engineering firm. County maps may be purchased at most Chamber of Commerces offices in a county or at the County Clerks office or at the Cooperative Extension office. Some book stores carry County maps also. **Keep a book on your big bucks and on your territory.**

Funnelling is often encountered in an area of unusually steep hills and deep valleys. When travel becomes too steep for comfort, your deer will tend to follow the line of least resistance and be funnelled by it into the bottom part of the valley. While they may prefer to travel up high, if it takes too much energy to do this they will follow that funnel of least resistance. That isn't to say, that if they are alerted, they will not break this rule. What it does say is, unpressed deer or deer moving on their own tend to follow the line of least resistance or the line with the most security; the funnel.

Water, river, creeks, and ditches are a chapter all by themselves. There is one last ploy sometimes used in the hunting of funnels; the trail block. Some veteran hunters will create their own funnels by blocking existing trails with brush or tree tops. This practice can move a big racked bruiser from an unhuntable run to one right up your alley. Plan ahead so they can get in the habit of using your trail.

Another off-the-wall practice that isn't used much for obvious reasons, is tying balloons on trees near the trail you want the deer to quit using. This works, but unless you clean up after the hunt it makes the woods look like a kids birthday party.

A still more subtle, but equally effective trick, is to pour human urine on the trail and surrounding bushes where you don't want the deer to travel. This works well, but if the practice becomes too wide spread in an area, it looses it's effectiveness and screws up everyone's hunting. In a heavily hunted area hard pressed deer will often times run right through a scent block situation.

FENCE ROWS

A fence row has become increasingly important in the day to day movement of the whitetail deer, especially the big bucks. Because wild fallow fields, where a big guy can lay up undisturbed all day, have become scarcer and scarcer due to clean farming. Those fence rows that still exist are doing triple duty. The triple duty is acting as a catch all for weeds. brush, and field debris, as boundary lines between property and territories and as day time bedding spots for hard pressed whitetails.

It was interesting to learn from some of our truly successful hunters , such as multiple record holder Fred Abbas, that they have encountered bucks also using fence lines as boundaries for their own territory.

When these fences serve as territorial boundaries the bucks in question will move up and down these boundaries in the patrolling of their territory. During the course of these territorial patrols the bucks will often cross back and forth over said fence. According to Abbas, it is at these crossing points or along the patrol route that a successful ambush can sometimes be made.

Because a fence can sometimes be awkward to cross, a deer will generally cross at a place where the fence is lowest or has been broken down. In fact there are places where deer through repeated use have caused a fence to develop a distinct sag. It is fairly easy to identify these spots of repeated use. Just look for bits of deer hair stuck in the twists of fencing wire.

A careful check of fence rows in your hunting area will also show where deer trails cross downed portions of a fence. These crossing points are excellent places to set up a stand. I learned, from one of Fred Abbas's many articles in the BUCK FAX MAGAZINE, that if the crossing isn't exactly where you want it you can tighten up the fence at the normal crossing place and release it at a place better suited to your use.

Fred Abbas and the buck he outsmarted
by changing the crossing point! Score 123.7

Keep in mind that this tightening and releasing must take place in close proximity to each other. It should also be done well before you hunt the area so that the deer can become accustom to using the new crossing. Fred did this once to better position a super buck and it paid off big time with a 123.7 Pope & Young winner. This buck, known as I.R.S.'s Buddy, crossed the fence and stopped exactly where Fred could make a perfect shot. One more case of an off-the-wall idea putting a wall hanger on the wall.

Some strains of whitetail bucks, generation after generations of deer in a particular geographic area, will develop an affinity for a certain type of bedding or resting area. Such is the increasing habit of big bucks in many

Michigan farmland hunting areas. They are shunning the woods and sticking to the fields and fence rows.

I know of one strain that has been using a specific group of fence rows for over 15 years as one of their daytime hide outs. We've used this knowledge several times to mount drives, and set up stands. Although it hasn't as yet resulted in a trophy kill, we have taken several lesser bucks. After all of this time and effort the "super bucks" still find a way to by-pass the drivers or standers. It's no wonder they have learned to trust this bedding area, it is almost unhuntable. I still have hopes that one of these days our plans will produce results, because there are two or three bucks in the area that will score 150 + Boone and Crockett.

We will also discuss the hunting method, I refer to as, hunting aside, again in our chapter on water, river, creeks and ditches, but the principle also holds true for fence rows.

We have found that big bucks like to lay off to the side of main deer trails and monitor the activity without actually being right in the mainstream. Understanding this habit and turning it into an off-the-wall tactic is known as hunting aside. When a main deer trail or general funnel follows an existing fence line or lane your biggest bucks will generally take up a bedding or watching position not on that fence or route, but 50 to 100 yards up a intersecting fence row.

In other words they will find a fence row coming in

from the side and take up position there, 50 to 100 yards from where it joins the main trail. When this intersecting fence row comes in from a higher elevation it becomes even more

Fences can also be very dangerous!

desirable as a resting/watching spot. If you use the "hunting aside" method your incidence of sightings, jumpings. and shootings should increase dramatically.

By paralleling the main trail or funnel 50 to 100 yards off to the side and being alert to the possibility that a super buck is laying up in every fence row you come to, you will hunt better, see more and hopefully be more successful. Believe me this is not for the faint at heart, because you will see bucks that will make your hair stand on end. This type of hunting can really juice up your season. Try it and be prepared to be SURPRISED.

SUMMARY
CHAPTER 2:
Woods and Weather; Fence Rows and Funnels

A. Big deer come from big woods.

B. Large blocks of unbroken land are always the home of at least one "super buck".

C. A county map, plat book and a note book are the tools of necessity for a big buck hunter.

D. Remember to always get permission from the land owner before you hunt

E. Deer seek shelter when a storm is approaching.

F. Hunting in wet/snowy/foggy weather can give you an advantage, use it.

G. Remember keep a book on your big bucks and their territory.

H. Funnels are either man-made or natural and cause deer to act in a predictable fashion when they encounter them.

I. By learning to identify funnels you can increase your chances of taking a true "wall hanger."

J. Learn where the funnels are in your territory and keep a book on your buck.

K. Get and use aerial photo's of your hunting
    territory.

L. Fence rows can act as funnels, hideouts, and
    territorial boundaries. Know and use them as
    helpful tools in your quest for an off-the-wall buck.

        Scout   Scout   Scout

WETNESS: RIVERS, CREEKS, DITCHES AND WATERS

T his chapter of OFF-THE-WALL, deals with water
and its strong influence in the daily life of a
mature buck. All deer need water to sustain life, but big
bucks use it for more than drinking, they use it as a tried
and trusted friend, a barrier of the first value against
pursuit.

To understand the fondness of deer for water you must
first examine the physical construction of its body. We
know that a deer's body is covered from head to hoof with
a dense hair, but did you know that this hair is hollow?
In the summer the hair is lighter and less dense, but still

hollow. In the winter it is much heavier and exhibits greater hollowness. Hollow deer hair is a very good insulator against the cold of winter, but it also makes the deer's coat a personal flotation device of the finest kind. In addition to the hollow hair there is also a great amount of air that gets trapped in the animals dense under fur. This buoyancy allows a deer to be completely at ease whenever they encounter wet footing and this in turn allows them to easily escape most predators, including us.

A river of this size won't even slow down
a determined buck, but it will leave his
pursuer's far behind.

For the past several years I have been the Editor for

BUCK FAX MAGAZINE, the official publication of Commemorative Bucks of Michigan, Inc., (CBM). This organization is officially recognized by the State of Michigan and responsible for the scoring and recording of all legally taken trophy deer. bear, elk and turkeys and the hunters who take them.

In addition to putting out 5 issues of BUCK FAX during each calendar year, containing facts, figures, and big buck hunter personal success stories, the organization has put out three record books containing all the trophy deer, bear, elk and turkey's taken since records have been kept.

If a person will take the time to study the CBM record book and plot the location of the most recent kills, certain common denominators crop up in almost every case history. Stick with me now and you'll soon see where we're going.

The most understandable of the common denominators is the physical condition of the area being hunted. In other words, the terrain in which the "big boys" are most often found and taken.

First of all you want to examine the records to find the most productive counties in terms of record book heads.

In Michigan this study will show several counties in the Upper Peninsula as constant producers of big bucks. It will also turn up five or six southern Michigan counties, one near Traverse City and the rest in the farm belt, that are currently leading the way when it comes to trophies. What do these geographically diverse locations have in common?

Matthew R. Usitalo and his 1992 firearm killed
Houghton County buck. Score 179.5. Ranked by
CBM as the #1 buck taken that year.

Number 1 is an adequate food supply, which allows a buck to take advantage of his superior genetic characteristics, those that allow him to grow extra special antlers.

Number 2 is a place in which he can elude the hunter

for 3 or 4 years and reach his top growth potential. Given enough food and protection, a genetically superior buck will reach trophy book size in three or four years and pass on his hereditary tendencies to an increasing number of offspring.

After studying these records of kills for the past several years here's what I think you should look for in a trophy hunting area. WATER!

Water is almost always included in the , "Big Buck Book of Tricks". He will use the waters, rivers, and drainages of his territory as his travel routes and boundaries, and when in trouble, as his escape routes.

Nearly all of the "bookies" taken recently had a lake, river, stream, creek, drainage system or wet swamp as the principle key in their daily movement habits. Along this piece of water or around it, you will find large chunks of non-productive agricultural land. This land will most often be in the form of almost unhuntable swamp. In the U.P. and northern Michigan this will be your traditional cedar swamp, while in the farm belt it is tag alders, cattails, saw grass, and just plain nasty wet second growth.

As we have said in an earlier chapter, if you can find a piece of land, especially in the farm belt, that has these characteristics and stretches unbroken for two or more miles, you have found the home of a record book buck; ABSOLUTELY!

Keep a book on your big bucks and know your territory!

How many deer shootings have you been involved in and the subsequent tracking jobs, that resulted in the quarry crossing or taking to water? A high percentage, I bet! When they are hurt they head for water. When they're pursued they use water as a relief valve. When they're in need of sanctuary, water is a trusted friend.

We know that a hurt deer will head for water to throw off its pursuers and to cool the burning of a wound, but did you know that a deer may also hide in the water? Did you know that they will lay right down in the water and let you walk by within only a few feet on the river or ditch bank?

No fair you say! Yeah, but it works for him and to out smart the trophy of a lifetime you need to know all of his tricks.

A couple of years ago, CBM record holder for Livingston County, Michigan, Terry Kemp, was conducting a one man drive along the edge of a flooded lake shore, towards two standers on higher ground. The object of the drive was a "super buck", known to inhabit that particular swampy lake edge.

Terry set his standers and made the drive. As he neared the end of his push he noticed one of his standers frantically motioning towards the lake. Thinking that his buddy wanted him to move more that way, he waded out in the brush until the water was nearly over his boot tops and finished the drive. Only a single doe bolted by within range of the standers, as a reward for his hard work. When he got up to his friends, he found out the reason for the frantic waving. It seems that from his elevated position the stander could observe the "super buck" entering the lake and swimming around Kemp with just its nose and antlers above water. Is water used as an escape route ? You better believe it!

Water protected places that big bucks like and use include - islands in streams, loops of a river that have water on three sides, islands in lakes, both inland and off shore. Part of the definition of an island is: something that is isolated by being surrounded by another medium; such as water. The key word is isolated, that is one of the reasons a "super buck" uses water as an ally, it isolates him from his enemy, you.

As a successful "big buck hunter" you can use this information to help you win the game of "Keep Your Antlers". Make his Off-the-Wall actions part of the solution to putting his antlers on your wall. **Keep a book on your bucks, get to know your territory and his!**

In my research for this book I have found that the single most used escape route by super bucks is the proverbial "ditch". This can be as small as two foot deep, to a real "hummer" with a bottom 30 feet down and awash with 6 inches of cool water. To prove the truth of this premise just get out there and check a few. You'll see from the tracks that these agricultural drainage veins are veritable whitetail highways. Chances are, that if you have a "super buck" in your neighborhood, one that has outlived his brothers, he will have one of these "ditches" woven into his life saving system.

Terry Kemp of Owosso and his
173.6 Livingston County buck.

As we said in the chapter on fence rows, the practice of "hunting aside" can and should also be used on ditches.

Most of your real "wall hangers" do not lay right along the main stream or ditch. They may use the main one for their travel route, but when they want to lay up and rest they will move 50 to 100 yards up a smaller side ditch. From there they keep tabs on the comings and goings along their back trail. If you show up following the main trail along the big ditch, "old mossy horns" simply slips out the back way and no one is the wiser!

In slipping out the back way he may use one of his novel abilities; crawling. Some people may doubt my word on this one, but it is a fact. I have seen it practiced and several of my friends report the same observation; deer are capable of lowering their bodies until their bellies touch the ground and then they literally crawl out of danger.

Hunting on a large wooded ridge, west of Big Rapids, Michigan, several years ago I was slowly working into the wind when a big doe came running thru the woods right at me. I already had my buck and was just still hunting/ driving for some friends who were stationed a half mile away to the West. When the doe was only 20 yards away she stopped and looked back, she obviously wasn't concerned about me. It is probable that she never even saw me. Looking in the direction of her stare I saw the back of an orange clad hunter leaning against a stunted oak tree. He was looking to the West and away from the stationary doe. The obvious reason she had stopped was, she had winded the stationary hunter.

Then a little to the South and between her and the

hunter, there came a spiked buck. When he was about 20 yards from the standing hunter he stopped. As he stood there, locked on point, looking at the stander, he began to sink down.

Within 2 minutes he was flat to the ground. With just his rear end a little elevated he slid around and crept away until he was 30 yards down the south side of the ridge and there he just disappeared. As he left one way, the doe continued on past me and across the road to my rear.

I was amazed that the hunter had not brought up his gun and fired, because that buck was in plain sight if he had only turned his head a little to the left. Taking my time and making a little noise, to alert the hunter, I walked up to his stand. I asked if he had seen the little spike. His reply was that he'd been there all morning and hadn't seen a damned thing. If a little spike, without much practice, can come up with a trick as slick as that one did, how much more skilled must a "super buck" be?

Dave Smith, a mid-Michigan barber and successful trophy hunter in his own right, related a similar instance that he observed just south of Owosso one day. Dave was working himself into position when he observed a buck and three does crossing an open area in back of a standing hunter, 100 yards away. Because the shot would have been in the direction of the other hunter and because it was a questionable shot at best, Dave just stood and observed.

As the animals drew closer to the stander the buck went into a full sneak with his belly smack dab on the ground. Because the ground was covered with waist high grass the buck just disappeared. The does just kept bounding along as if they were the only deer within 10 miles. As far as the standing hunter was concerned that's exactly what he thought; he never even knew there were 4 deer until they crossed a fence way out of range.

Deer not only sneak and swim they also stand on their hind legs to see over the tops of corn stalks. We'll cover that in the chapter on farm land crops.

One last sneaking story. About 4 years ago I stumbled on a fence row that big bucks liked to lay up in when moving from one territory to another. It just so happens it is huntable by two persons and especially easy for a handicapped hunter such as myself. What I do is drop off my hunting partner near one end and I drive down 300 yards to the other end and park my truck. Then I get out and lean against the front or sit on the tail gate.

This overgrown, wide and weedy fence row, with a shallow ditch in the middle, in good years separates a corn and stubble field. The only time I hunt this field is at the end of November, when all of the crops have been harvested.

This past year, as I was driving by one day, I noticed two bright yellow rubs on bushes next to the fence. Ah-ha, it was being used and my oldest son was going to be home for Thanksgivings the following week-end. I anticipated a real opportunity for us to renew our hunting vows and maybe get a real "hummer" for the buck pole.

It was a beautiful, crisp November afternoon when I finally dropped my son off at the up end of the fence and took my place at the side of the lower end. Once I was in place, Mike started slowly through the grass and weeds, keeping a sharp eye peeled for any movement. Any shot that was to be taken was to be taken by me. Mike lives in Kentucky and didn't buy a Michigan license that year.

A third of the way down a big deer broke to the right and stopped in the cut corn field. A doe. Now right down the fence line came another deer running hell bent for election. Up came the gun and I waited for an open shot.... nuts it was a smaller doe. She blew by me at no more than 10 yards. What a chance, if it had been a buck!

I guessed that the "old man" must not have been at home, until I caught my son waving. While I had been busily checking out the "ladies" he had come out of the left side of the fence row on his belly, crawled across the stubble field and high tailed it over the next plowed field. All I saw was the north end of a south bound buck, with a butt as wide as a Hereford's and with a rack to match.

This "super buck" had used two off-the-wall tricks to completely bamboozle me. He used the doe decoy ploy to get my attention and the belly crawl to get out of range. I felt so foolish, because if I had just seen him I would have had a nice clear 100 yard shot. But, even when I looked his way I didn't see him crawling thru that 12 inch stubble. Sometimes even the best laid plans....You know .... happens!

Before we got sidetracked down the sneaking path we were talking about water. Let's pick up where we left off.

Streams, rivers and creeks are used by deer much the same as ditches. They are whitetail highways and by-ways. Their banks provide food and shelter. Their cooling waters provide relief from the heat and a thirst quenching goodness. As we have stated before they act as funnels and as escape routes.

When a pursuing predator comes to a sizeable stream or river, they are usually stopped for a few moments, while they figure out a way across. Not the whitetail, they are in and out in a moment, gaining that precious lead that spells survival in the short, as well as in the long run. Because water does not carry the scent, but instead washes it away, a dip in the creek or swim in the river, is an important advantage. Especially when your pursuer is using it's nose in trying to turn you into a meal.

The whitetailed deer has for centuries been using water in this way. Even now, when his principle enemy no longer uses it's nose for tracking, the deer still looks to water as it's number one friend, in time of need. **Keep a book on your buck. Know his area.**

In a very wet bottom area, the "super buck" will seek out and find a slightly raised area, in it's deepest recesses and may wait there the entire season. They have been known to just sit tight and let the does come to them.

When you have a dominant buck that is using these tactics, he is often considered as unhuntable. However, if you are a "super hunter", such as Mitch Rompola, of Traverse City, Michigan, you turn this to your advantage. Confronted with this type of buck, Mitch just goes right in after him, he hunts him on his own turf. This takes a special kind of dedication and skill, but the rewards are as Mitch states them, "Fantastic."

Mitch Rompola and his #1 Michigan Bow kill.
Score 181.9

Rompola has 10 in the records book, including the #1 bow killed typical for the state and there are at least another 10 he hasn't even entered. To make it even more remarkable, all of these "super bucks" were taken with a bow. Mitch Rompola is truly a "super hunter" who has learned to hunt big bucks, off-the-wall! He will tell you, that you should scout three (3) times as much as you hunt. If you will only believe and follow this advice you too may take an Off-the-Wall biggie!

Paul Mickey, of Saginaw, Michigan, the State's record holder for the #1 non-typical whitetail with a firearm, has learned to hunt big whitetails in cattail marshes. Where waders are as much a part of the uniform as a bow or a gun, Paul takes on these big boys in their very damp bed rooms and comes home a winner, time after time.

Paul Mickey and his 238.2 point #1 Michigan Non-typical

Wet willies to the contrary, Paul's invasion of a thought to be unhuntable terrain, has proven off-the-wall bucks can be taken if you will use your head for something other than a place to put your hat. With more than 10 "super bucks" in the CBM Record book, Mickey, has shown that he is a "master hunter", whether the deer are wet or dry!

Knowing that a big buck uses a particular drainage system or wet spot will not guarantee you a shot, but it, along with other information will increase your odds. I can not stress enough; **Keep a book on your bucks**. If you don't you will come to a place where you have a critical habit of this buck in your head, but you cannot recall it. After he pulls a sneaky on you and gets away you will say, "I knew he used that trick, or that escape route before, but I just forgot." Don't get caught with your brain out of gear! **Keep a book on your buck and put him on your wall!**

It's not always good enough to know where or how, water is used in a big bucks bag of tricks. Some special tips on using water to help you hunt him, I believe, are now in order.

A "super buck", actually any buck for that matter, sees water as his friend, he doesn't expect danger to come by water. You can use this to your advantage. There are places where unbridged or unbridgeable stretches of water provide a protective back door to a large pieces of whitetail country. The deer know from experience that danger always comes from the land side and they therefore put the river or water at their backs.

You can take advantage of this by floating the river in a boat or tube. Some places this approach can be accomplished by wading the stream in waders. There are also times when just being able to use a boat, to get across into otherwise unhuntable territory, will do the trick.

The use of a fishing float tube, a pair of light waders and a handgun in a shoulder holster has and will continue to give some resourceful trophy hunters that extra edge needed to fill their deer tags.

In my many years with CBM I have noticed that a significant number of record book bucks have come in from along southern Michigan's larger rivers. Those river's have the cover along their banks or cut through those places that just naturally hold big bucks. In questioning many of the successful hunters a common thread exists in their hunting method; they float. They float in with a boat or canoe and shoot the big guy's without them even knowing they were around. Pure and simple, they catch them with their backs turned and their eyes closed, completely unaware of approaching danger.

Crossing a large lake to a side that is otherwise unapproachable, is another slick way to put you in trophy territory. A boat also gives you an easy way to bring out your wall hanger.

The margin of a beaver pond is
another good place for super bucks!

Because deer like and often use water, they occasionally make a lot of noise when passing through it. Knowledgeable bow hunters who are looking for an opportunity at the big buck in the area will often place their tree stands near a trail through flooded timber. Wearing boots and going well back into the wet woods gives them several advantages. Number one (1), deer don't expect hunters where the ground is covered with water. Number two (2), you can hear the deer coming. Number three (3), there is almost no competition from other hunters. Number four (4), the biggest bucks in the area normally choose this type of terrain as one of their hide outs.

Water can make us uncomfortable and water can cause us problems, but water can also be the key to putting those off-the-wall bucks on your wall. **Be sure you keep a book on your buck.**

SUMMARY
CHAPTER 3:
Wetness: Rivers, Creeks, Ditches and Waters

A. Water is a tried and trusted friend of the big buck.

B. A deer's body is well adapted to a life in and near water - hollow hair/buoyancy.

C. Deer use water not just to drink, but as an escape valve and daily protector.

D. Michigan big buck hunters traditional take most record book "biggies" somewhere near water. Every buck taken had water somewhere woven into his daily routine.

E. Find a stretch of land unbroken by roads and containing a piece of wet nasty land and you have found the home of a record book buck; absolutely!

F. Expect a buck to use water and know where the water is in your bucks territory. **Keep a book on your buck!**

G. If you have a "super buck" in your area the chances are great that he uses a ditch as part of his life saving system.

H. Hunting aside is an excellent approach to catch a wise old ditch buck.

I. Keep your eyes peeled for that belly crawling buck. They can and do crawl.

J. Water doesn't slow down or bother a deer at all!

K. Super Hunters know and use water to their advantage. Hunting big bucks in the wet stuff may be off-the-wall, but that's why they are so big.

L. Use water to your advantage, it can give you the edge you need.

M. Keep a book on your bucks, know your territory!

Scout   Scout   Scout

Roads, Highways and By ways

R oads, highways and by-ways have been with us since we were born and since our quarry, the whitetail buck was born. We use our roads to get from place to place. The whitetailed buck crosses our roads to get from place to place. As we have said before, a deer cannot travel from one spot to another without leaving tracks. The first, finest and most obvious place to find deer concentrations is at the location they cross a road.

I've heard it said, that you cannot tell a buck's track from a doe's. But you can tell a big deer from a small deer by the size of their tracks and that is the first thing to look for. Big bucks almost always have big bodies and almost always leave big tracks, look for these marks of passage along the roads in your hunting area.

Deer in the Midwest are wherever you find them and that's all over. Trophy bucks are present in every county of the State of Michigan, even heavily populated Wayne County. While I can't tell everyone exactly where the deer are located in their territory, I can tell you, if you will follow these simple directions you'll soon have a handle on their whereabouts.

What the experts do is take long quiet drives in the evening, just looking. They're looking for deer or tracks crossing sand or gravel back roads or on the shoulder of black top roads. In the winter a fresh snowfall can give you wonderful clues as to a deer herd's habits.

A deer crossing this big is a dead give-away
that, this is a prime spot for big bucks!

Another outstanding use of the road is to make your trips to and from work along as many back roads as possible. I have seen some truly amazing deer by traveling roads parallel to the main ones. Not only does that give you two scouting trips per day, but it helps get you mentally ready for the day. To me 30 MPH on a secondary road looking for deer just beats the hell out of 65 MPH on a super slab. You might have to start for work a little earlier, but the easier, mind freeing travel of the back roads, just makes that a sacrifice worth taking.

One summer morning 6 years ago, just before day light, while taking a less traveled blacktop, I caught a group of 4 bucks, led by a big non-typical, sneaking across right next to a bridge abutment. I had never suspected that deer crossed at that location, but subsequent checking revealed a sometimes used trail that may yet result in an off-the-wall score. It is just one more bit of information in my book on this particular "super buck." **Remember, keep a book on your bucks.**

You really don't need a car to check out these road crossing bucks, because a bicycle or a motor cycle works just as well. As matter of fact, before I lost the use of my left leg, many a days jogging turned up hoofed evidence near my home in Michigan. Surprisingly, some of the biggest tracks were very close to the edge of town.

Record book bucks don't get big by being stupid. The bigger they get the more nocturnal they become, a fact we will discuss later on. Besides becoming creatures of the shadows, they also develop travel habits that are very different from the run-of-the-mill whitetail. A case in point is their handling of road crossings, particularly expressways.

Chances are a deer that makes a habit of crossing an expressway in the conventional manner, in his day to day wanderings, is not going to live to the ripe old age that produces a large rack. However, there are plenty of whoppers that spend their entire lives within the sound and sight of these "super-slabs" and still live to reach bragging size.

There are crossings like this
all along our freeway system!

How do they do it? First of all, they seldom cross over the highway, they cross under it. That's correct, they walk through culverts, from one side of the road to the other.

How they develop this habit is open to conjecture, but I do know that bucks like to travel along the bottom of drainage ditches and I suspect when one of these crosses under a road, the deer just continues on through to the other side. Thus, a habit is born.

Another more reliable way this habit is learned is by following a lead doe who has developed this peculiarity. It is also a fact that younger bucks will follow and understudy a "super buck" and thereby learn all of the big guys secrets. Just this past year one of our successful local gunners was telling me about a big buck he shot that seemed to come out of nowhere along with a doe and a smaller buck. Because he was hunting near where a good sized ditch crosses under an X-way I ask him if they could have come up from under the road? A look of amazement crossed his face and he said bye- golly that probably is where they came from. I went on to tell him that I had long suspected that the big bruisers in the area were crossing under the X-way at that point, but could never get permission to hunt there and prove it. Well, he had permission and now has a 160 + wall hanger for being at the right place at the right time.

I personally, have observed this under the road crossing happening three times and I suspect it is done a lot more than we might think.

To prove to yourself the truth of these statements, just walk one of the many roadside ditches along an express way in known deer country. You are going to be surprised at the depth of these ditches and by the number of tracks along their bottom. Most of these ditches are so deep that a deer can travel for miles without being seen at all from the road. When they do come to an intersecting ditch and with it a culvert under the road, they have a ready made crossover.

In doing research to prove or disprove this theory, I have stopped and examined many such ditches and culverts. I kid you not, 100% of these tunnels had deer tracks in them. You may not know this, but we are not just talking about your common big tin tubes under the road. We are, in most cases, looking at a one or two chambered concrete structure, either side of which is large enough to allow the passage of a car.

Several of these watery passageways consisted of one wet side and one dry side. The dry side was covered with tracks of all kinds and obviously only carried water during flood time. Check it out for yourself. A stand near one of these subterranean crossings could yield you a shot at that neighborhood "super" buck, you never knew existed. **Keep a book on your bucks and know his territory!**

This next dissertation on highways and roads includes some material, which has over the years raised an eyebrow or two. Right-off-the-bat, I want to say that I know what the law is concerning the hunting of expressways and road right-of-ways. I do not advocate the breaking of those laws.

However, the whitetailed deer is no respecter of man's

laws and there are many times when you are going to be hard pressed to outwit him, especially when you are up against his natural ability and societies laws.

When we build large expressways across miles and miles of prime hunting territory we create a man made barrier to the free roaming wild game. Many, many game animals are eventually killed on these roads by our swift moving vehicles. Millions and millions of dollars and not a few human lives are lost each year in these accidents. And yet some notable off-the-wall bucks make their primary homes in the wide medians of these same highways. How do we hunt these median monsters?

Suggestion #1: Determine, if at all possible just where this "super buck" has his highway home. Number 2: Scout the land/fence row paralleling this hide out and determine his escape route and entrance route; he will have more than one. Be especially careful that you pick the best one. If the land along either side of the "super slab" is privately owned, secure permission to cross it to look for sign and if possible, get permission to hunt at the same time.

Number 3: Once you have secured all of the afore-mentioned information, do the following: Purchase a orange plastic bag such as you see being used to collect trash along State highways. Drive the section of highway containing your buck's hide out and see which organization, if any has undertaken to clean up that piece of road. Call that organization and see when they are scheduled for a pick up day. If that day is during deer season, volunteer your help. During the cleaning up operation be sure you cover the section where your "super buck" is known to hide.

Could it be a big bucks secret hide out?

Number 4: Bust him out of his bed, being especially observant as to which side of the road he runs. Number 5: take up a stand just off from the road right-of-way on that side of the road and wait for his return; you should get a shot if you have done your homework.

Number 6: If there is no organization assigned to clean up that piece of highway, park your car at the closest bridge and make it YOUR piece of highway. Clean up the junk and maybe you'll clean up on whitetails. Remember it is illegal to carry a gun or bow while you are in that median; trash is OK.

Number 7: I suppose you could drive slowly down the shoulder in a pick up truck, with a strong armed buddy in the back. As you approached the suspected hide out you could have him throw rocks into the area , hopefully scaring the big guy out into huntable territory. Using this scenario you might get a ticket from the state trooper's for littering or reckless driving. At the least, the "bunny hugger's" are going to report you for animal harassment.

Number 8: Remember back a few pages, to that discussion of ditches and culverts. If a ditch or culvert breaks out in the middle of a median and most do in those wide median areas where bucks take up permanent residence, the closest tight cover to that ditch either up or down the X-way is the place to expect the big guy to lay up. Nine times out of ten he will be using that culvert to cross under the highway.

Number 9: Use your imagination, you probably can come up with a legal tactic that will accomplish the same results; congratulations, you've outwitted an off-the-wall buck.

Remember, keep a book on your buck!

SUMMARY

CHAPTER 4:
Roads, Highways and By ways

A. Roads are a valuable tool when looking for and finding the location of an Off-The-Wall buck.

B. Express-ways are fine, but a slow drive on a back road can turn up more big buck possibilities and its good for your nerves besides.

C. Use your drive time to Scout, Scout, Scout.

D. Deer go under as well as over highways.

E. Walk some roadside ditches, you'll see that they are veritable whitetail highways.

F. The medians of our X-Ways hold some truly gigantic bucks.

G. Use your imagination and you may come up with a legal tactic that will place one of these off-the-wall median bucks on your wall.

H. **Remember, keep a book on your buck.**

Scout   Scout   Scout

Man-Made-Monuments

F irst of all, I'll make a list of the Man-Made-Monuments known to attract big bucks and known to have an influence in the game of Catch A Horn! Following that listing I'll explain their significance. As you read this list, be sure to add in the note section any other 3M's you might think of.

Cemeteries, golf courses, school grounds, colleges and universities, parks, towns and villages, camps, nature preserves, airports, resorts, reservoirs, military reservations and bases, hospitals and manufacturing facilities.

The first time I ever thought of the idea for this book

it was in conjunction with a story I wrote for a local paper and later used in the Buck Fax Magazine. It was a story called Off-The-Wall and it was about a "super buck" that had been using a little cemetery about a quarter of a mile from my old Michigan farm.

It seems that this 11-point, 225 pound biggie was nocturnally covering the fields and farms for several sections around until morning approached. At a few minutes to sunrise, "old bucky" would slink down my back fence line and slip quietly into the old overgrown graveyard and sleep away the day. This graveyard was not over an acre in size and only held a dozen or so graves.

Because it was seldom used any more and only cleaned up once a year, our ghostly whitetail was almost never bothered. In as much as his comings and goings were almost always in the dark and his approach was through the crops at the rear of the cemetery, this Off-The-Wall deer grew big and undetected for years.

One morning my neighbor, who farmed most of the land thereabouts, was out in back of his barn very early looking at a piece of equipment he was going to need later in the day. Luckily he caught sight of "old bucky" slipping in the back door of the marble orchard.

Now, Ron was a veteran deer hunter and his tag was as yet unfilled. His first urge was to grab the gun and go get that deer, but wisdom prevailed and he waited until dawn of the next day. Come 7 am the next morning, our hunter/farmer was sitting on a pail in the fence row leading past the south end of my hay field and he collected the biggest Off-The-Wall buck taken that year in our part of Michigan.

That little graveyard is just one of many that dot our country. Many of these small cemeteries are overgrown and half forgotten, the perfect hiding place for a big buck who does most of his stuff at night. A little investigation could make one near you, the final resting place for the biggest trophy of your life.

A cemetery sanctuary of the first order!

Because graveyards are places that most people steer clear of, you should have very little competition and almost no problem with visitors screwing up your hunt.

Little cemeteries are not the only final resting places that big bucks pick to hide out in. Some of your largest suburban and metropolitan places of internment actually have resident populations of deer. These ghoulish whitetails may spend all of their days among the head stones and venture out into the countryside only at night. In some of these graveyards, I have even heard that the caretaker feeds the animals on a regular basis. Upon reflection, hospitals also fall in this category.

From personal experience, I know that these cemeteries seldom have deer-tight fences and that most deer lead double lives; those on the inside and those on the out. A wisely selected stand near one of the deer's coming out spots could put an awesome rack over your fireplace sometime soon.

Golf courses are another semi-public place that deer hang around. You may seldom see them on the course during the middle of the day, but early in the morning and as darkness approaches, the lush fairways and close cropped greens become favorite feeding and playing places for more furry critters than you might think. It is a strange course indeed that doesn't have at least one or two wet/wild corners that are almost never visited by errant golfers. It is these places that may harbor the biggest buck you have ever seen.

If you go to the greens keeper of your neighboring golf course, you might get permission to hunt the edges of the course after regular playing hours. Keep in mind that these same deer you are interested in might be doing a lot of damage to the course in their nighttime excursions. Damages can run the gauntlet, from torn up greens to antler scarred trees. You would probably be doing the course management a favor by thinning out the whitetail population. Don't tell anyone else about your plans or the competition will become unimaginable.

At the last Michigan Deer Spectacular, I heard of a Cheboygan County non-typical, that was poached by an employee of a local golf course and which scored 198 Boone and Crockett. Needless to say, the bowhunter who was working on that wall hanger was just sick when he learned that his intended was shot from a golf cart with a rifle during bow season.

Once again, golf courses are seldom fenced with deer-proof fences, so stands along the edges make for interesting and often productive hunting. The big non-typical mentioned above lived out most of his life in a mid-course pothole. Such is the way of many Arnold Palmer infected deer. Idea: A trusted friend with a 5-iron and a few old balls could just spook that special buck right out past you if you teamed up at the right time of year.

Schools, universities, colleges and seminaries are normally places where hunting is not allowed, particularly with firearms. However, these same institutions almost always have large and small pieces of unused land that could and does hold some excellent whitetail bucks.

I will be the first to tell you, I don't have all the answers when it comes to ways of hunting this type of land. Just read on and use your mind; that's what we're trying toimprove! The more you exercise your brain cells in the pursuit of Off-The- Wall bucks the better you're going to become at it. You're going to begin to think like a big buck and the next time you see an off-the-wall situation you will come up with an off-the-wall solution. Bingo, your wall will be the resting place for the rack of a lifetime.

If a school's property is located in the rural part of the land and if it is not posted, it is sometimes alright to hunt upon this land; local customs prevail. Some blocks of school land are not even used for normal school functions and are reserved for agricultural classes. Check with the local Ag. instructor for permission to hunt. Invite him along. It might just be the thing it takes to open up a special spot, a spot where the big one lurks.

Seminaries are different. Because they are privately funded, they might allow one or two quiet, well mannered archers to hunt the fringes of their lands.

Colleges and universities are a different story. Check with the Department of Public Safety at the school and have a specific spot where you want to hunt. Keep your request to archery only as the use of firearms will almost always be denied. If the answer is no, limit your hunting to the area around the perimeter of the school grounds. Sometimes, small, one or two man drives using unarmed drivers can accomplish the desired results. Most schools, regardless of size, will tolerate one or two persons walking thru their grounds, just don't make an issue out of it.

Towns, villages and cities are notorious for banning all hunting within their boundaries. When this happens there is little you can do but relegate your hunts to property that adjoins said town. If you can locate the hangout of a "super buck" within town, take up a stand where he is apt to exit the city limits on his nightly excursions and be waiting. Be patient, because some of these urban hummers are the stuff dreams are made of.

My son recently picked up a set of shed's scoring in the 170+ range only 300 yards from the center of a 50,000 person urban Michigan city. The deer are often in and around cities because they have learned it is safe. Your only real chance is to locate their hideouts and wait at the edge of town for them. Remember, they do not spend their entire lives in town.

Parks, reservoirs and nature preserves are much the same as towns and villages and should be approached the same way. The only difference is that parks, reservoirs and nature preserves may hold more deer than towns. The edges may also be easier to hunt.

Camps and resorts fall in the same category, but are normally privately owned. There are many camps and resorts throughout the Midwest that encompass hundreds of acres and contain deer herds in the hundreds themselves. Most of the time these locations are closed to hunting, and while they may not have deer proof fences around them, the pure size of the property means that the big bucks residing there seldom have to leave the property.

Some of these resorts allow guests to hunt on the property for a fee. If you can afford the cost, this is sometimes a good way to get a crack at a known trophy buck. I would explain, this type of hunting is not for everyone, but neither is it hunting captive deer. There are no deer proof fences around these properties and the deer are free roamers, therefore legal candidates for trophy recognition.

On the other hand, most camps will not normally allow hunting on their property, but when the deer herd grows to the point that it is ruining it's range, the camp management may declare an open season. This is normally done once every 8 to 10 years and to be allowed to participate in one of these hunts is a chance of a lifetime.

I know of one father and son team that was chosen to take part in one of these open hunts. It was on the property of a religious camp in Northern Michigan and both father and son came home with beautiful bucks. The son's buck was so good that it still stands as the all time typical record for the county that the camp is located in.

Airports, military reservations and bases are locations that may contain sizeable deer herds and where occasional open seasons may be declared. Airports are more apt to allow selected hunters to take deer on their property in a more controlled manner because of the danger to aircraft. If you want an opportunity to take part in this controlled harvesting you should contact your local airport manager and let him know you are a responsible hunter who would abide by any rules that he may deem necessary. There is an off chance that you could get a crack at a truly remarkable buck.

More than one 10-point has been seen at the
end of this mid-Michigan runway!

Under the classification of military reservations and bases also comes the federal and state wildlife reservations. In the State of Michigan, where I live, there are several locations that fulfill those classifications. Perhaps the most widely known such areas are Fort

Custer near Battle Creek and the Shiawassee Flats Federal and State Wildlife Preserve south of Saginaw.

Both of these facilities allow hunting by permit, and in a good year, your c. ances of taking a "super buck" are excellent. Hunts on these reservations are generally staggered to allow bow hunters and gun hunters separate chances at the abundant game.

I've had the opportunity to take part in several of these hunts and consider the opportunity as one of the highlights of a long and exciting life hunting big game. The sheer number of big bucks seen and the many missed opportunities just make a hunter want to shout with joy—THANK YOU GOD, THANK YOU FOR THE CHANCE! A hunt like this is what America must have been like when Lewis and Clark went West!

Contact fort or preserve officials early in the year for information, because the few available permits are sometimes given out early in the year.

Manufacturing facilities have a history as checkered as any, especially with regards to allowing hunting on their property. Where a large corporation holds big pieces of property for future use, they will sometimes allow employees access for hunting. On the other hand, this prime whitetail habitat is often kept for the private use of the Head Kahuna.

In the case of the General Motors Fisher Body Plant at Grand Blanc, Michigan, the excess property to the north of the plant that used to be part of a World War II tank testing ground is entirely enclosed with a deer proof fence.

Watching this randy GM buck gave
me some fine info on rutting bucks.

Within this enclosure are about 100 of the nicest whitetails I have ever seen. With frontage on old U.S. 10, the public can observe these deer year around. There are also tremendous opportunities for area photographers to take some great photos. I've done so myself on occasion.

As you might guess, deer in this situation are pets and the management of the plant guards them closely. However, a captive herd such as this does afford local hunters the opportunity to view the interaction of the species and might provide them with a good tip-off as to when the rut was to start. As far as I'm concerned, any opportunity to watch whitetails in action is time well spent.

When trying to gain access to plant property you know or suspect contains a shootable trophy , first of all make an appointment with the owner or plant manager. If you can get in to see this individual, and get his cooperation, the battle is won. Realistically, your chances are probably slim, but nothing really worth the effort comes easy does it?

If the answer is no, see if you can get his permission to follow a wounded deer on to the plant property if you should shoot one on adjacent land. Now, secure permission to hunt the land next door. Do as I have suggested for other next door hunting projects and you could still get a crack at an off-the-wall biggie that spends most of his time on unhuntable land!

All man-made-monuments are not of steel and concrete. Some of these are old domestic domiciles gone to rack and ruin; abandoned farms, etc. A drive down almost any back country road in whitetail country will turn up one or two of these aged, tumbled down farmsteads; those dreams of yesterday nestled in long brown orchard grass.

For some time, I've been aware of the propensity of big mature deer to seek out day beds in long brown orchard grass. Deer may not reason as we do, but somehow they instinctively know that the tall dead grass found around old buildings gives them an added advantage in the game of, "Keep Your Antlers."

Deer that use the tall grass around old, little used farmsteads do so for a couple of reasons. With a little study, we can understand these reasons and perhaps turn them to our advantage. Number 1: People shy away from disturbing the area around one of these relics of an earlier day because they think the place may be haunted. Number 2: It may be that they are afraid of what may be lurking in the tall grasses, such as old rusty nails, broken bottles, old machinery or abandoned wells; we can only guess. Whatever the reasons, once one of man's monuments is abandoned and grass starts to grow, people just stay away.

The perfect combination for a big buck;
abandoned buildings and long grass!

When the people leave, the varmints soon move in, and not much later the first wise whitetail will sneak a quick nap in the deep, warm, brown, protective grass. If you are careful to keep the noise down and the wind in your favor, you can get some really close-in shots at what could potentially be the next Pope & Younger for your county.

One of the other limiting factors in this type of hunting is the number of times you can hunt an abandoned farmstead. As with other specific whitetail cover, a big trophy buck will only tolerate being surprised once or twice, during any season before he quits using a site altogether.

As James Bond use to say," Once is an accident, twice is a coincidence, and three times is enemy action." Most off-the-wall bucks draw the line at "Once".

Again, you need to be forewarned, because some of these bucks are going to bail out with as much commotion as a flushing ring-necked rooster. You will probably ventilate more ozone than buckskin, but it surely will be an experience you won't soon forget.

If you are very careful of the wind and make no noise, you may catch a snoozer before he knows his napping spot has been compromised. That, my friend, is a very special accomplishment. Any deer hunter worth his or her salt considers catching a deer asleep a major fulfillment. To achieve this is to say you have graduated as a stalker. It may also put your name in the record book, particularly if the buck you out maneuver carries the head gear normally associated with long grass ruins. **Remember, keep a book on your buck, this year's mistake could be next year's success!**

The girls, as well as the guys, put big ones on the wall. Just ask Nancy Hyypio of Chassell, Mi. She dropped this tremendous 17 point, 220 lb. trophy near her home in the U.P. during the 1991 firearm season.

SUMMARY
CHAPTER 5:
Man-Made-Monuments

A. Cemeteries

B. Golf Courses

C. Schools

D. Parks

E. Towns and Villages

F. Camps

G. Nature Preserves

H. Airports

I. Military Reservation and Bases

J. Hospitals

K. Manufacturing Facilities

L. Old Abandoned Farms-Deep Brown Orchard Grass

M. **Keep a book on your buck, so you don't make the same mistake twice.**

Scout   Scout   Scout

CROPS

Until I got well into the preparations for this book, I didn't think a chapter devoted to crops and their use by "super bucks" would have been relevant to our cause. I was wrong.

Because so many of our "super bucks" now live in close proximity to farmable land, that buck's relationship with crops is very important if we are to understand his total lifestyle.

In the far northern part of the whitetails range, Northern Minnesota, Northern Wisconsin, Michigan's Upper Peninsula and the Northern part of Southern Michigan, the deep forest (cedar swamp) is the secret retreat of most "super bucks".

This magnificent 7-point came from the
depths of a Schoolcraft Co. cedar swamp.
Tom Van Riper, of Durand, was the successful nimrod.

In the farm belt of these same states and in those whitetail states to their South, the big cornfield has replaced the tangle of cedars as the off-the-wall buck's surest hideaway.

If you have ever tried to separate a determined buck from his 80 acre cornfield, you will know what I mean when I say, "a very difficult job for an army of less than 20 men!" Up until a couple of years ago, I would have said, "Impossible."

The few times that I tried cornfield hunting, the results were always the same. I saw deer, but they also saw me. There was something missing from my technique. I knewthat there could be deer in the corn fields, but I was always surprised when I saw one. What I seemed to lack was confidence. No one, that I knew personally, had ever taken a big buck from a cornfield. Oh, sure, they had picked off the occasional critter going to or coming from the maize , but a true, deep penetration corn field score was not something I was familiar with.

Let me be absolutely honest. The biggest excuse my Southern Michigan hunting friends use for not getting their deer is, "they haven't picked the corn yet!" That's right. You can't get one of those hat rack hunks while they're in a standing 80 acre cornfield. Hell no! It's just like they're in a 4 mile long cedar swamp. The guys around here say, "Wait till the corn is down and then we'll fill our freezers." Until then, they stick to hunting the rut lines and potholes, or they go North and hunt the big woods bucks.

There have been, from time to time, articles that described techniques for hunting fields of standing corn, but I wasn't sure that those purported methods worked, that is until I read a story that I included in Commemorative Bucks of Michigan, Inc., 1993 Fall Issue of the Buck Fax Magazine. Entitled, **Corn Field Hunt**. It was by Larry Faught of Lapeer, Michigan.

Larry's story, in his own words, describes his hunt for a known, non-typical "super buck" which spent most of it's time in or around corn fields. Larry told the story in such a gripping manner it became at once one of our most commented on pieces. Not only did our readers enjoy the story, but for the first time, I understood how a successful hunter went about hunting the supposedly unhuntable corn fields.

Larry's prescription for corn field success is: Take only what you need and travel light. Soft, quiet clothing; wool, acrylics, fleeced clothes is a must. Because you can't help but make some noise going thru a corn field, a windy day helps create a lot of extra noise that will help cover your movement.

Rainy days are also good days to hunt corn fields. You'll make very little noise. Snow covered ground makes seeing deer in the corn rows much easier, but it also makes it easier for you to be seen. This is a trade off you'll have to decide for yourself. Faught took his big non-typical on a cold, snow covered day in November with a 10 to 20 MPH wind blowing.

Move slow. Ease your head through a row so you can look down it one way, then the other, always looking across as many rows as you can see through just in case you walk right to one. Now, step through the row and repeat the process again. With the wind in your favor, slowly move perpendicular across the rows.

Depending on how quiet you can be and how noisy the corn field , this will determine your speed. Larry says that one day it took him 1 1/2 hours to cover a field, and the next time the same field took 2 1/2 hours. He emphasizes, SPEED IS NOT WHAT YOU'RE SEEKING.

Larry Faught and his very special
cornfield non-typical.

Once you have located a deer, back out of the row and retrace your steps 5 or 6 rows, moving only when the wind permits. Calculate the distance down the row you saw the deer and move quietly and slowly in that direction, once again moving only when the wind permits. When you get close to where you figure the deer to be, stop and start looking for whitetail body parts.

Chances are that you will only see bits and pieces of your quarry, so at this point care must be taken in picking your shot. If you still cannot get a clear shot try moving, as the noise of the wind permits, into a better shooting position. By this time your heart should be beating a mile a minute and the hair on the back of your neck standing straight on end. Congratulations you have just successfully hunted an unhuntable corn field buck!

There are several other types of farm fields that deer seem to prefer, but corn is the only one that requires a special hunting method. Because most annual crops are normally harvested by the time deer season rolls around, you will probably be faced with mostly picked or plowed fields.

Occasionally, you will run into a soy bean field that has not been picked by the first part of October. Even with unpicked bean fields the only added equipment that you need is a pair of binoculars and some good walking shoes. Because many of these fields are vast in size with no natural obstructions to mar their symmetry, a good glassing from a easily achieved vantage point should reveal any bucks laying up in them. Once you have determined that there is a "shooter" in the field, the real work begins.

Bean field hunting is much like shooting antelope out West. You must plan your stalk or drive so that you are where or close to where the buck will exit the field. A reminder: some states do not allow hunting soy bean fields while the beans are still on the plants. Most of these deer when spooked are going to head for the closest wood lot or drainage ditch. Working yourself into position in the ditch or woodlot, no matter how far away, is probably the surest way to harvest one of these off-the-wallers.

The same tactics that worked for hunting bean fields should also work when your odd buck takes up residence in a long grass field. These fallow fields seem to hold a certain fascination to big deer, similar to what we discussed in the chapter on Man-Made-Monuments. Because they blend in so well and because the grass and weeds are often longer than the deer are tall, just determining they are in there is the biggest part of the problem.

Scout the edge of the field to determine where the deer are entering and exiting the field. Pay special attention to where the closest food source is. Now, hunt the field as if it were an unhuntable piece of property. Actually getting into and hunting the field itself is nearly impossible. Any shot you will get will be a "jumper" and they'll disappear so fast that the only gun to use is a 12 ga. shotgun with Double-OO Buck. Personally, I have no fondness for this load because it is a great crippler. It may work alright when your prey is a charging lion or a 10 yard away buck in real thick stuff, but if you must use it, make absolutely sure you take no shot over 20 yards.

The best way to put one of these "long grass loners" on the wall is to catch him going and coming or to get some of your friends and drive him out to waiting standers. **Remember, Prior Planning Prevents Piss-Poor Performance and keep a book on your buck!**

Orchards and/or tree farms are the last special crop situation we will deal with. I know there are other crop layouts that may require special tactics, but I have never run into them, and if you do, just adapt one of these plans to your particular problem. If you come up with a new and novel way to put a "wall hanger" on your wall, please let me know and I'll include it in the next issue of CBM's, BUCK FAX MAGAZINE.

A Christmas tree plantation can
provide some real opportunities if you
can get permission to hunt there!

As with bean field hunting, orchards require binoculars or a spotting scope. First, you must locate the deer within the orchard and then plan your attack. Driving works if you have enough hunters, and a well thought out and conducted stalk can be equally rewarding. Again, knowing and watching favorite entrance and exit points is also a good strategy.

Before you go into one of these orchards, be sure you get permission from the grower. There is nothing a farmer likes any less than some irresponsible Ya-Hoo filling his precious trees with lead. The plus side of this asking first is he may tell you right where the deer lay up. Tree farmers and fruit producers have a lot of problems from deer eating on their trees and the bucks using them for rubbing posts. Very often you will be welcomed if you ask in a nice way.

SUMMARY

CHAPTER 6: Crops

A. Many of our "super bucks" now live in close
   proximity to growing crops.

B. The big cornfield has replaced the cedar swamp
   as the number one holder of trophy deer.

C. Larry Faught's cornfield hunting method really
   works.
   1. Slow and easy
   2. Use the wind
   3. Quiet clothes
   4. Patience
   5. Speed is not what you are seeking!

D. Bean Fields

E. Long Grass Loners

F. Orchards

G. Prior Planning Prevents Piss Poor Performance

        Scout   Scout   Scout

Odds and Ends

I n the preparation of this book there was much that didn't fit in just one or another of the chapters or that was not a topic large enough to take up a whole chapter all by itself. Odds and Ends is the place these little tidbits of information are going to be enshrined or buried as the case may be.

CONVERSATIONS

One of the very special ways in which you can increase your chances at an old wall hanger is by listening to conversations between proven veteran trophy hunters. You must listen for what is left unsaid as much as to what is said. In other words, read between the lines when listening in on these talks.

One of the great advantages that myself and other CBM members get from belonging to the organization is in sharing ideas or just plain listening to conversations between big buck hunters.

I personally have never sat down and listened to a conversation between CBM Vice-President Mitch Rompola and another successful trophy hunter that I didn't gain some new insight into big buck hunting. These repeatedly successful big deer hunters have learned some very special ways to locate and take whitetailed bucks.

While these "whitetail wise men" don't just run around telling everyone they meet their secrets, once they get into a conversation with another serious seeker of "super bucks", wisdom is there to be had for the careful listener.

The next time you go to an outdoor function where hunting is being spoken, hang around and listen as much as you look. What you hear may just put that big one on your wall by this time next year!

NOCTURNAL

The idea that when a big buck goes nocturnal, ie: moves only after dark, he is unhuntable has been around for a long time. Unfortunately, this idea has gained a lot of credence lately, and more and more good hunters have given up on these "wall hangers" that love the dark of the moon.

Mark Ritchie and his #1 Michigan typical
all weapons buck. Score 186.1 B&C

I don't know that I have all of the answers, but let's just kick it around. When a buck deer reaches the ripe old age of 3 1/2 years, he starts to grow his best head gear. Along with this great set of antlers comes a place of authority within the whitetail family. He is now bigger, smarter, and older than 97% of all the other deer. That's a fact. Just to live to be 3 1\2 years old as a buck deer in the State of Michigan makes you special.

The buck on the right is definitely in the top 3%.

Instinctively, this group of elders shuns the company of lesser deer except at the breeding time. Sometimes in the velvet months of July and August, these big brutes will share their feeding and resting places with other big bruisers. It is at this time of year that we stand the best chance of learning there are such animals.

Long cool evening drives down the back roads and sand trails, being ever watchful along the edges of crops and hay fields as the sun sets, are your best bets for sightings. Always carry a good set of binoc's or a window attachable spotting scope. These big guys may be three fields back or just at the far edge of a 80 acre bean field. Good optics are a must. However, knowing there is one or three off-the- wall bucks near where you hunt goes a long way towards helping you harvest one come fall.

I only got to see this guy once, in June.

It is true that when September comes and the first squirrel hunter enters the woods or the first pat hunter busts a hull, our trophy bucks will go nocturnal. That is one of the ways they got to be trophy bucks. There's nothing so mysterious about that. It's just a fact.

Now, let's be wise. That "super buck" did not disappear from the face of the earth. EVERYTHING HAS TO BE SOMEWHERE! Your buck is somewhere! All you have to do is find him and outsmart him. That is what this book is all about, finding and outsmarting the wisest and luckiest deer on the planet.

Hopefully by this point in the book, you will have exercised your mind to the point where you are thinking like a wonderful, wise and wacky whitetail. Now, do what most hunters refuse to do. Get off your 'duff' and go hunt him on his own turf, using what you have learned so far. You will soon find that the nocturnal buck is not unhuntable. Scout, Scout, Scout, THEN HUNT!

ETHICS

There is more to trophy hunting for whitetails than hanging a large set of antlers on the wall.

Each hunter will ultimately decide for himself the method that gives him or her the most satisfaction, but generally speaking, it is a one-on-one confrontation between a single hunter and his chosen quarry.

In other words, the hunter meets the trophy buck on it's own turf, with the odds in the favor of the buck, and comes away successful. It's the hunter who decides whether success was achieved or not.

Success may simply be the outsmarting of the buck with no shot taken, or it may be a successful photo, or it could be, and usually is, the good shot, the subsequent tracking, collecting, processing, mounting, and scoring of a record class whitetail.

But, let's not kid ourselves. All of the above is meaningless unless it is done within the legally and morally acceptable guidelines set forth by the State and your fellow hunters.

If you break the law in the taking of a trophy buck, you are a crook, plain and simple. Both you and your deer of a lifetime are tainted and all of the joy associated with your success is for naught. Because that deer is "dirty", you should not be able to enter it to be ranked with all of the other legally taken "biggies". Most of us understand this and abide by the rules. That's an important part of being a deer hunter.

The younger hunters among us may not hear us talk about it much, but to take the life of an animal as special as the whitetailed deer is a very important act. It is not an act to take lightly, and many of us upon achieving success bow our head or drop to one knee and thank our God for allowing us that success.

After all is said and done, a few words of thanks for making our hunting year complete seems somehow appropriate. It isn't so strange. It's just what our brothers, the American Indian, did. When they made a kill, they thanked their God, Manitou, for a successful hunt! A real hunter knows that if the God of the hunt is not smiling, then success will be many arrows away.

When you kneel beside your next trophy buck you should see out of the corner of your eye Old Daniel Boone and Davy Crockett standing there with smiles on their faces. If for some reason they are wearing scowls of disapproval, you have let down the traditions of the hunt and need to mend your ways.

Your responsibility is to be the kind of hunter Fred

Bear or Jack O'Conner would be proud to share a hunt with. That means being fair, honest and proud to be a hunter of the whitetailed deer!

A true trophy, even if I only took it with a camera!

SHINING

When I grew up in the State of Michigan the mere act of shining was considered tantamount to violating. Where I got that idea I don't exactly know, but when one of our north woods relatives said, "Let's go shining," they usually came back with some wild beef in the back of the pickup. That was then and this is now. We have a law in Michigan that says you can legally shine before 11 PM up until the month of November. During the month of November, no shining of any kind is permitted. Period.

Because our trophy whitetailed bucks tend to go nocturnal after September, the use of a spotlight to locate them after dark should be one more important tool in your arsenal of tricks. When you are out there shining, be very sure that you do not have any kind of weapon in your vehicle. To have even shells from a gun can sometimes result in your arrest; they (the Conservation Officers) will believe that you threw the gun out the window before you were stopped.

Yeah, that's right! You're going to be stopped because many shiners take the shining opportunity as a chance to get a buck that they don't legally have the talent to take. My friends with the Department of Natural Resources figure one in every three shiners is dirty, and therefore, one out of every three stops should result in an arrest.

Maybe that's why I don't go shining more often than I do, I just can't get over thinking it's illegal. But, don't let this fear stop you. Shining is a good way to sample the big buck pool in your area. It is also a lot of fun. I suppose you can imagine how much fun I used to have with a 80,000 candle power light, two six packs of beer, a pack of Marlboro's and my best hunting buddy in the old four wheel Jimmy. Wow! We sometimes unwound so far that we couldn't even go to work the next day. It's too bad those good old days are gone, and remarkable that I lived through them!

Please respect our farmer friends and during your evening of shining, don't run those big lights across their living room walls. Also, keep your lights out of their barnyard because this makes them damn mad. This type of thoughtless behavior turns them against all hunters and we need their friendship if we are to continue to enjoy the out-of-doors.

All off-the-wall experts are not old and grizzly. This 125.6 P&Y was taken by first time hunter James Bower, age 13.

SCENT

There are whole books out there that deal with the art of scent use and misuse. I have read many of them and tried their suggestions. Scents work. When used at the right time and in the correct manner, scents can be a deadly part of a hunter's off-the-wall arsenal.

Trust me on this one; human urine from a male is not a good substitute for deer urine. There are those who ought to know better that say it doesn't make any difference. Moose Muffins! I once decided to refresh a scrape with a little of my used water; it was the biggest scrape around and had been in use for years. After I left my mark it was never used again! Male human urine scares wild deer. They know it's from a predator, their enemy, man!

On the other hand, female urine, especially when the lady is at or approaching the height of her menstrual cycle, has a certain exciting affect on rutting bucks. One of the oldest of the scent secrets is to collect your wife's used sanitary napkins or tampons. These are then placed in close proximity to your stand and when "Old Horny" comes to call, you ventilate his lecherous hide.. This does work, and even burying them at good spots seems to work also.

Another scent tip is used to position a buck once you have him coming your way. Let us say that you have a very special spot in which to shoot your dream buck, but the secret is to get him to stop in exactly the place where you can shoot. Bury some scent in just the place you want him to stop and lower his nose.

Either place a combination of your favorite scents in a small used sour cream carton and bury it under a few inches of dirt, or take an old film carton and place this level with the ground. Fill the carton with cotton and add several squirts of your favorite scent product. In either of these scenarios, when your buck comes along, he should at least pause and lower his head to check out the scent. He may not stay long, so be ready to shoot. Bango, you've got your off- the-wall buck!

There is nothing quite like the real thing!

My last tip on scent is, collect the tarsel glands from each buck you shoot and save them in a plastic bag in your freezer. Next year, when making a mock scrape in your "super bucks" territory, bury one 4 inches deep right in the middle of the scrape. If all goes well, this should guarantee repeated visits from the boss buck. It should turn a fake scrape into a real barn burner.

BLINDS

There are hundreds of deer blinds on the market. Some are for up a tree and some are for on the ground. I've been using one for in a fence row, that you can make easily by yourself. Either get an old piece of 4 or 5 foot high farm fence 8 feet long or a piece of large square welded wire the same length. Into this piece of fencing, weave straw, hay, corn or grass until you are obscured when seated behind it.

Once your weaving is completed, cut shooting holes or slits in it so that from a sitting position you can easily shoot through. Now, when you need to create the perfect blind somewhere along your big buck's fence row trail, all you need do is attach it on an existing fence and sit on the other side. I have also used this type of screen to fix up a blind in the corner of a field where two fences come together. It is very cheap and very natural.

A real good one, built by Bob Sattler of Owosso.

KEEP A BOOK ON YOUR BUCK

All through this book I've been telling you to keep a book on your buck. That's because it is so important to your success.

OK, here is how I would do it!

Purchase several 4 x 6 spiral notebooks, or better yet a package of 6 x 9 inch steno books. I believe these come four to a package.

When you become familiar with one buck, or at the start of the season, begin to keep notes on the deer and area you are in. Keep these notebooks in your hunting car, and each time you return from hunting, without fail, jot down what you learned or what happened during that hunt. Include such things as where you parked, how you entered the land, how many deer you saw and where. Draw little maps showing the deer trails and special terrain features. On these maps indicate rubs, scrapes, fences and funnels.

Indicate from which direction the wind was coming and what the weather was. Be sure and mark down the time you started and the time you finished. Also, along with recording the deer you saw, indicate the time you saw them and where they came from.

This is just a partial list to get you started, but once you are under way, I'm sure you will add more information. Now, each time you get ready to hunt, reread your notes. You may just reread them on that area or on a particular buck you are hunting, but never overlook this preparation. Remember the 6 P's and add the three S's.

Prior Planning Prevents Piss Poor Performance and
Scout, Scout, Scout!

Good Luck !

The End

SUMMARY

CHAPTER 7: Odds and Ends

A. Conversations...listen more than you talk, there is wisdom to be had.

B. Nocturnal

    1. Many big bucks grow old and grey by moving only at night.

    2. In the summer, when the big guys are in velvet may be the only time of year when you get an angle on a trophy biggie.

    3. The nocturnal buck did not vanish, everything has to be somewhere.

    4. Think off-the-wall, use your head.

C. Ethics...You and only you can decide what is right and what is wrong. You must be responsible if our sport is to continue to exist!

D. Shining...A way to find the home of an off-the-wall winner or a way to end up in the "slammer". Do it right or don't do it at all.

E. Scent...It really works when you take the time to learn how to use it. Use it, but don't abuse it!

F. Blinds...There are the good, the bad, and the ugly. Keep it simple!

G. Keep a Book on Your Buck...Know and understand his territory. Remember the 6 P's...Prior Planning Prevents Piss-Poor Performance...

Scout   Scout   Scout

and THEN HUNT

Bibliography

Bertalan, Dan. *Bowhunting's Whitetail Masters,* Stackpole Books.

Rue, Leonard Lee III. *Whitetails,* Stackpole Books.

Smith, R. P. *Deer Hunting,* 2nd ed. Stackpole Books.

Smith, R. P. *Tracking Wounded Deer,* Stackpole Books.

Smith, R. P. *CBM's Michigan Big Game Records,* 1st, 2nd, 3rd ed. Smith Publications.

Van Riper, Jack. *BUCK FAX MAGAZINE,* CBM Publication, Volumns 11, 12, 13.

Wensel, Gene. *Hunting Rutting Whitetails,* Gene Wensel Publisher.

Index

Future Books By
Jack Van Riper

In the Curwood Tradition...
A collection of ten short outdoor/environmental/
adventure stories. Great reading for young adults
and older fans of the late James Oliver Curwood.

Along The Chippewa Trace...
A year in the life of an outdoor writer along the
rivers and streams of Central Michigan.

Notes

Notes

Notes

Notes